Stations of the Cross for the Sick

By *Catalina Ryan McDonough*

Illustrated by *Mary C. McDonough*

Our Sunday Visitor Publishing Division
Our Sunday Visitor, Inc.
Huntington, Indiana 46750

In Memoriam: Bishop James T. McHugh
1932-2000

Nihil Obstat
Rev. Monsignor Anthony A. LaFemina
Censor Librorum

Imprimatur
✠ Robert J. Baker, S.T.D.
Bishop of Charleston
September 15, 2002

The Scripture citations used in this work are taken from the *Catholic Edition of the
Revised Standard Version of the Bible* (RSV), copyright © 1965 and 1966 by the
Division of Christian Education of the National Council of the Churches of Christ
in the United States of America. Used by permission. All rights reserved.

Every reasonable effort has been made to determine copyright holders of
excerpted materials and to secure permissions as needed. If any copyrighted
materials have been inadvertently used in this work without proper credit being
given in one form or another, please notify Our Sunday Visitor in writing so that
future printings of this work may be corrected accordingly.

Our Sunday Visitor Publishing Division
Our Sunday Visitor, Inc.
200 Noll Plaza
Huntington, IN 46750

ISBN: 1-931709-82-3 (Inventory No. T47)
LCCN: 2002113416

Cover and interior illustrations by Mary C. McDonough
Cover design by Tyler Ottinger
Interior design by Sherri L. Hoffman

PRINTED IN THE UNITED STATES OF AMERICA

Preface

This portrayal of the Stations of the Cross by Catalina Ryan McDonough brings the Passion, suffering, and death of Jesus to us in a very relevant and personal way. The author delves deeply into Jesus' humanity and reveals it as our own.

We imagine how Jesus felt when condemned to death. Through our illnesses many of us have received a similar sentence; we feel the weight of the cross as we struggle with the challenges that each new day brings. When we fall, we must get up, as Jesus did, and continue our journey, wherever it may lead us.

Nearly three-and-a-half years ago, I was diagnosed with advanced prostate cancer. Since then I have seen many new treatments come on the market, and many more are on the horizon. I have watched two of my children graduate from college; my last will graduate this year. I have lost friends to this and other diseases and wondered why them and not me. I have heard of patients near death who have made astounding recoveries.

We don't know what the future holds for any of us. In our times of quiet desperation we find comfort in knowing that we are not alone. We draw courage from Christ's victory over death. We embrace the power of hope through prayer.

I brought all of these thoughts with me when I prayed these Stations. In the prayers and meditations contained in this small book, I found a real connection to the journey of Jesus through His most difficult times. I can imagine His anxiety, His pain. At the same time I am touched by His compassion for others on the way to Calvary when He is the one who is suffering so. I am moved by His forgiveness of those who brought Him there and His love for them.

Jesus never lost sight of His mission. He didn't quit or give in. He didn't complain. He remained faithful to the end. Jesus was a great

3

teacher during His life, and through His Passion and death He teaches us how to approach death.

Jesus completed His journey with dignity and great courage. We know we must complete ours. Each of us has at least a few more "stations" to go, but we know we will have Jesus with us for the rest of the way. We have His example and His assurance that He will be there for us.

I am quite sure that these Stations will be read, pondered over, and deeply appreciated, not only by the sick but also by all people who seek a deeper connection to the Passion of Jesus Christ. I am thankful to Kitty McDonough for her insights into our Lord's Passion, evident in the meditations you hold in your hand, and thankful that my brother, Bishop Bob Baker, asked me to reflect on them.

May the Holy Spirit enlighten you as you pray them!

Jim Baker
Solemnity of Pentecost
April 19, 2002

Introduction

The Stations of the Cross have had universal appeal for centuries. When the Franciscans took custody of the sacred places in the Holy Land in the year 1342, they also took on a special mission to promote devotion to these sites and the Passion of Jesus Christ. Eventually such devotion went from the holy sites to monasteries, friary chapels, and eventually to parish churches throughout the world.

Popes such as Innocent XI, Innocent XII, Benedict XIII, and Clement XII helped to promote this devotion and extend it. At present one can obtain a plenary indulgence each day when, under the usual conditions, one makes the Way of the Cross.

I am happy to promote this devotion by introducing this unique presentation of the Stations of the Cross by Catalina (Kitty) Ryan McDonough. In addition to focusing her life on raising a family, Kitty has worked alongside her husband running a family business, taught art and English at community colleges, and written a fair amount of poetry. She has taught CCD to first graders and served as eucharistic minister at Our Lady Star of the Sea parish in North Myrtle Beach, South Carolina.

A friend of Kitty's presented a draft of these meditations to me, and I immediately saw the value of her labor of love. Kitty wrote these Stations when a dear family friend, Bishop James McHugh, informed her family that he had been diagnosed with cancer. Bishop McHugh had led the American bishops in efforts on behalf of the cause of life and had served as bishop of Camden, New Jersey, and Rockville Center, New York.

Kitty had spoken by phone with Bishop McHugh when he was at Memorial Sloan-Kettering Cancer Center, and she found him to be brave and utterly prepared for God's will. The night after her conversation with him she slept poorly, got up at 4 a.m., and began writing these Stations.

Having a brother of my own facing cancer courageously, I could identify with Kitty's desire to provide a series of reflections for someone suffering, based on Jesus' own agony. What better source of strength can there be for people who are ill and suffering than that afforded by Jesus, the Son of God, facing such obstacles? Uniting their struggles with Him and His, their crosses become His and are easier to bear. He is bearing crosses on His shoulders out of love for them. That is one of the messages of this little book of meditations.

I treasure the beautiful remarks that Archbishop Timothy Dolan makes in his book *Priests for the Third Millennium* (Our Sunday Visitor, 2000) about Father Gene Hamilton, the New York priest who died at the age of twenty-four, two hours after his specially approved ordination to the priesthood. Young Gene Hamilton had been struggling valiantly with cancer with the enduring conviction that all that really mattered was "Christ, and Him crucified." Archbishop Dolan indicates that one of Gene's special devotions during his hospital stays was the Stations of the Cross.

At the end, without the strength to reach the chapel, Gene would shuffle down the corridor of the hospital, dragging his IV and oxygen, and stop at fourteen different hospital rooms, designating each of them one of the stations, recognizing in each cancer patient the suffering, bleeding Savior on the *via crucis*. To Gene Hamilton, his life had meaning, purpose — his suffering was salvific — if united with the Passion and death of Jesus.

May those who struggle and suffer from any illness find healing and hope as they reflect on the meditations and pray the prayers they find in these *Stations of the Cross for the Sick*.

✠ Robert J. Baker
Bishop of Charleston
Good Friday, March 29, 2002

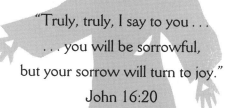

"Truly, truly, I say to you . . .
. . . you will be sorrowful,
but your sorrow will turn to joy."
John 16:20

Prayer to Saint Raphael

O Raphael,
Lead us toward those we are waiting for,
those who are waiting for us.
Angel of happy meeting,
lead us by the hand toward those we are looking for.
May all our movements be guided by your light
and transfigured by your joy.
Angel guide of Tobias,
lay the request we now address to you
at the feet of Him on whose unveiled face
you are privileged to gaze.
Lonely and tired,
crushed by the sorrows and separations of life,
we feel the need of calling you
and pleading for the protection of your wings,
so that we may not be as strangers in the province of joy,
all ignorant of the concerns of our country.
Remember the weak,
you who are strong,
whose home lies beyond the region of thunder
in a land that is always peaceful,
always serene and bright with the resplendent
glory of God.

I.

Jesus Is Condemned to Death

MARK 1:9-11

In those days Jesus came from Nazareth of Galilee and was baptized by John in the Jordan. And when he came up out of the water, immediately he saw the heavens opened and the Spirit descending upon him like a dove; and a voice came from heaven, "Thou art my beloved Son; with thee I am well pleased."

We adore You, O Christ, and we praise You,
because by Your holy cross You have redeemed the world.

~

ord, You stood before Pilate, alone and condemned. Betrayal had brought You to this place.
Now we begin the Stations of the Cross, feeling alone and
betrayed by our bodies, which once had served us well.
With this stage of our sickness, whatever its name, we
come to the reality of death in a new way. The Passion has
begun. It is Yours, it is ours. Stay with us, Lord, help us to
see Your will in our sickness as in our health. From the
moment the priest poured baptismal water on us, we have
belonged to You, and You have been well-pleased when we
have done Your will. We pray for more priests to help generations grow in the faith that enables us to recognize You
on this road. Lord, be pleased with us now in our efforts to
walk the path to Calvary. ✝

II.

Jesus Is Made to Carry the Cross

LUKE: 9:23-25

And he said to all, "If any man would come after me, let him deny himself and take up his cross daily and follow me. For whoever would save his life will lose it; and whoever loses his life for my sake, he will save it. For what does it profit a man if he gains the whole world and loses or forfeits himself?"

We adore You, O Christ, and we praise You,
because by Your holy cross You have redeemed the world.

~

Lord, You have spoken to us in paradox: Dying we live, losing we win, the least is the greatest, the blind will see . . . we struggle to recall all that we have been taught, all that has been revealed to us, so that we may eagerly accept our cross. Feelings washing over us now are so painful; they feel exactly like a cross. But You have promised that the yoke is sweet, and Your burden light. Lord, we cannot bear it without Your help. It is so new and strange, crushingly heavy. Lord, stay with us as we move forward each day of this journey. ✝

III.

*Jesus Falls
the First Time*

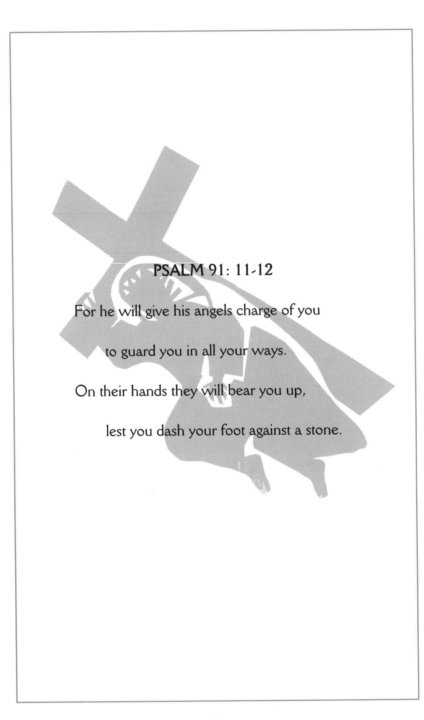

PSALM 91: 11-12

For he will give his angels charge of you

to guard you in all your ways.

On their hands they will bear you up,

lest you dash your foot against a stone.

We adore You, O Christ, and we praise You,
because by Your holy cross You have redeemed the world.

ord, we ask of You that in the rush of these new thoughts and experiences, we may hear also the rush of angels' wings. With faith, and it is a gift, we can bear anything. Increase our faith, Lord, as we confront the tumult of emotions: fear, anxiety, concern for people and things we must leave behind, our loved ones, our work, our bodily strength, our beautiful world, and yes, those flawed relationships that can never be repaired fully on earth. We fall under all this. Lord, help us, pick us up as You picked Yourself up when You first stumbled and fell on the road to Calvary. ✝

IV.

Jesus Meets His Mother

JOHN 19: 26-27

When Jesus saw his mother, and the disciple whom he loved standing near, he said to his mother, "Woman, behold, your son!" Then he said to the disciple, "Behold, your mother!" And from that hour the disciple took her to his own home.

We adore You, O Christ, and we praise You,
because by Your holy cross You have redeemed the world.

We think of our own mothers. If they are still on earth, they must suffer with us, and we would spare them if we could. If they have passed from this world, we are comforted that we may see them again. But we wonder: What is it like after death? Will we know our loved ones? Speak to them somehow? We are filled with questions, if not doubts. Where can we turn? To Your mother? You gave her to us when You were dying on the cross. Mary is with us now, as she was with You then. Mother of God and of mankind, pray for us sinners now. ✝

V.

Simon Helps Jesus Carry His Cross

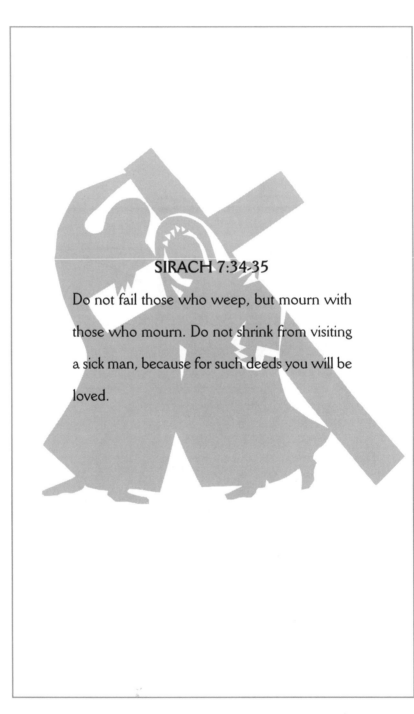

SIRACH 7:34-35

Do not fail those who weep, but mourn with those who mourn. Do not shrink from visiting a sick man, because for such deeds you will be loved.

We adore You, O Christ, and we praise You,
because by Your holy cross You have redeemed the world.

ord, once we were like Simon, minding our own business, with a job to do and the health to do it. Simon came into town on some errand of his own, when suddenly he was caught up in a terrible event, plucked from the crowd to help carry a cross for a stranger on His way to crucifixion. Yes, that's how it was for us, living an ordinary life when suddenly You drew us to Your side with the gift of sickness, asking us to carry Your cross a little way with You. Yes, now we share in your Passion, and other Simons come forth to help us on the way. We are grateful for them, and we want the grace to be grateful for this gift of our share in Your Passion, which is now ours. ✝

VI.

Veronica Wipes the Face of Jesus

ISAIAH 50:4-5

The Lord GOD has given me the tongue of those who are taught, that I may know how to sustain with a word him that is weary. Morning by morning he wakens, he wakens my ear to hear as those who are taught. The Lord GOD has opened my ear.

We adore You, O Christ, and we praise You,
because by Your holy cross You have redeemed the world.

Nurses, technicians, doctors, and hospital workers all have the opportunity to become Veronicas in this passion of ours. Some have developed a professional manner that is more businesslike than compassionate, and we pray for them. Others have become the Veronicas who dare to look deep into our eyes, to see and sympathize with the suffering they encounter in us. For them we thank You, Lord, and for them we pray as they step forward bravely, to ease our pain with the pure and tender fabric of their own humanity. ✝

VII.

*Jesus Falls
the Second Time*

JOHN 6:57-58

"As the living Father sent me, and I live because of the Father, so he who eats me will live because of me. This is the bread which came down from heaven, not such as the fathers ate and died; he who eats this bread will live for ever."

We adore You, O Christ, and we praise You,
because by Your holy cross You have redeemed the world.

hen we find ourselves humbled and brought low by this cross we share with You, it is the eucharistic ministry that gently draws us up again. To our bedside, in the hospital, or at home, You come to us through these men and women. In that sacred moment when the eucharistic minister withdraws the consecrated Host from that little pyx, You are present visibly to cheer us on; receiving You in this Holy Communion, we can rise again, take up the cross, and follow You. Thank You, Lord, for the mercy of this ministry. ✝

VIII.

*Jesus Speaks
to the Women*

JEREMIAH 31:8-9

"... the woman with child and her who is in travail, together; a great company, they shall return here. With weeping they shall come, and with consolations I will lead them back, I will make them walk by brooks of water, in a straight path in which they shall not stumble; for I am a father to Israel..."

We adore You, O Christ, and we praise You,
because by Your holy cross You have redeemed the world.

ike the women of Jerusalem who wept as You neared them on the road to Calvary, our family, friends, and neighbors are moved at the sight of our suffering. They know that someday they, too, must walk this path, and in their hearts they weep for themselves and their loved ones, fearful of the dark side of Your gift of the cross. Your only recorded words on the road to Calvary were to the weeping women: "Do not weep for me, but weep for yourselves and your children...." Their simple tears moved You with such compassion that You found the strength to speak to them. Help us, Lord, to feel compassion for those who witness our daily struggle. ✝

IX.

Jesus Falls
the Third Time

PSALM 90:1-4

LORD, thou hast been our dwelling place
  in all generations.
Before the mountains were brought forth,
    or ever thou hadst formed the earth and
      the world,
    from everlasting to everlasting thou art God.
Thou turnest man back to the dust,
    and sayest, "Turn back, O children of men!"
For a thousand years in thy sight
  are but as yesterday when it is past,
  or as a watch in the night.

We adore You, O Christ, and we praise You,
because by Your holy cross You have redeemed the world.

Lord, three times you have fallen on the road to Calvary; three times Your feet have failed You. But You are the Everlasting Now. Sharing in Your Passion, we will not count the times we fail You; we only beg You to lift us up each time. Lord, if we recover from this illness, let us keep the closeness to You that the present trial has brought us. We place our trust in You, dear teacher, so we may see Calvary with gratitude in our hearts, no matter when or where or how we come there, where You are waiting for us, all love and mercy. ✝

X.

Jesus Is Stripped
of His Clothing

JOHN 21:18

"When you were young, you girded yourself and walked where you would; but when you are old, you will stretch out your hands, and another will gird you and carry you where you do not wish to go."

We adore You, O Christ, and we praise You,
because by Your holy cross You have redeemed the world.

ord, since this sickness began we have endured many invasions of the body's privacy through tests, consultations, treatments, or surgery. How painful it is to submit to the ministrations of others. But before us You stand meek as a lamb, while soldiers have stripped the garments from You. One by one we must shed the layers of false pride or true, of health and vigor, and of many worldly favors. Just let us keep that loincloth of faith, and yes, a sense of humor in the midst of our humiliations, so that we may step up to the cross clothed in Your grace. ✝

XI.

Jesus Is Nailed
to the Cross

PSALM 91:14-15

Because he cleaves to me in love,
I will deliver him;
I will protect him, because he knows
my name.
When he calls to me, I will answer him;
I will be with him in trouble,
I will rescue him and honor him.

We adore You, O Christ, and we praise You,
because by Your holy cross You have redeemed the world.

When we gazed at the crucifix as children, we marveled at Christ's wounds, at the drops of blood on His brow and the wound in His side. Nailed to a cross! One prayer book used words that have lasted a lifetime: "Even when I am pricked with a pin..." Nailed to a cross! Kids are accustomed to pinpricks, to scrapes, bruises, and scabs from falls on the playground. Nailed to a cross! He did that for us! Lord Jesus, help us accept the physical and mental pain of our sickness as You accepted the nails in Your hands and feet. Comfort us with the awe we felt as children, and give us the awe-filled understanding that Your Calvary is ours now, and You are with us every inch of the way. ✝

XII.

Jesus Dies on the Cross

JOHN 12: 31-32

"Now is the judgment of this world, now shall
the ruler of this world be cast out; and I, when
I am lifted up from the earth, will draw all men
to myself."

We adore You, O Christ, and we praise You,
because by Your holy cross You have redeemed the world.

ord, You came to the world as paradox, the Word made flesh. Now the paradox that we must die to live is enacted on the cross. Your mother, Mary, and your apostle John are at the foot of Your cross suffering with You. Help those who stand by us in our last hours. Help us to forgive those who have hurt us, and forgive us our failures to love. From the cross You forgave; help us to do the same. Give us the grace to accept joyfully the death that approaches, whether it comes to us alone or in the presence of loved ones. Bring us past that cry of "Why have You abandoned me?" to the final "It is finished," when You will embrace us eternally. With the good thief we say, "Jesus, remember me when You come into Your kingdom." ✝

XIII.

Jesus Is Taken Down from the Cross

LUKE 1:46-49

"My soul magnifies the Lord, and my spirit rejoices in God my Savior, for he has regarded the low estate of his handmaiden. For behold, henceforth all generations will call me blessed; for he who is mighty has done great things for me, and holy is his name."

We adore You, O Christ, and we praise You,
because by Your holy cross You have redeemed the world.

Your lifeless body has been placed across Your mother's knees. The human woe of the dead Son returned to His mother's arms expresses all that can be imagined of sorrow. Mary had known since the presentation of You as a child in the temple that she would be pierced with sorrow, but she could not have known how, until it happened. Not only does she endure and accept, but she loves us all, sinners though we are. So we pray: *Holy Mary, Mother of God, pray for us sinners, now and at the hour of our death.* Mary will stand by us, as she stood by You, at the foot of the cross. May Our Lady take us by the hand when our hands are still at last. Mediatrix and Mother, place our hands in those of Your Son. ✝

XIV.

Jesus Is Laid in the Tomb

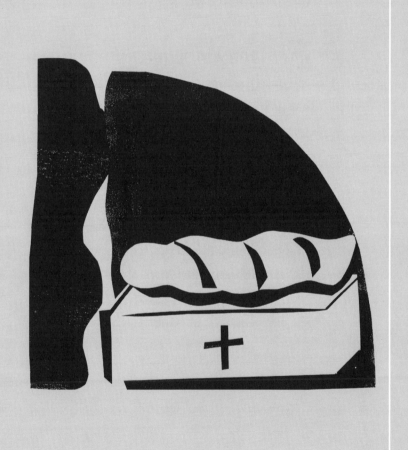

PSALM 90:14-17

Satisfy us in the morning with thy steadfast love,
    that we may rejoice and be glad all our days.
Make us glad as many days as thou hast
        afflicted us,
        and as many years as we have seen evil.
Let thy work be manifest to thy servants,
        and thy glorious power to their children.
Let the favor of the Lord our God be upon us,
        and establish thou the work of our hands
        upon us,
        yea, the work of our hands establish thou it.

We adore You, O Christ, and we praise You,
because by Your holy cross You have redeemed the world.

ord, resurrection is the key to all we believe and understand of our faith. The sorrow of Your mother and friends as the stone is rolled into place will be changed to joy at Easter. We pray now for our families and friends to see beyond interment to the glory that awaits us. Even our silent graves give praise to You, Lord, for You will gather all on the last day. When all that remains of us is our names, etched in granite, cast in metal, or on the tongues of those who loved us, help us to remember that You knew us in our mother's womb before we were named. Our journey begins and ends in You, Father Creator, Son whose Passion we share, and Holy Spirit through whose gifts we make this prayer. Amen. ✝

Prayer of Saint Simeon

⁓

Come, true light.
Come, life eternal.
Come, hidden mystery.
Come, treasure beyond name.
Come, ineffable reality.
Come, inconceivable Person.
Come, beatitude without end.
Come, never-setting light.
Come, unfailing hope of all those who must be saved.
Come, O mighty One, who always does all things
*   and recreates and transforms by your will alone ...*
Come, my breath, my life ...
My joy, my glory, my unending gladness,
*   come.*

Prayer of Saint Thomas More

⁓

Thank you, dear Jesus,
for all you have given me,
for all you have taken away from me,
for all you have left me.